Sunset

Creative Decorative Painting

Stenciled walls and a table stenciled with the same design
make a feature of a dull hallway.

SUNSET PUBLISHING CORPORATION ■ MENLO PARK, CALIFORNIA

Published in 1993 by Sunset Publishing
Corporation, Menlo Park, CA 94025
by arrangement with
J.B. Fairfax Press Pty Limited

First Sunset Printing August 1993

Editor, Sunset Books: Elizabeth L. Hogan

Library of Congress Catalog Card Number:
93-84317.
ISBN 0-376-04298-2.
Lithographed in the United States.

J.B. FAIRFAX PRESS PTY LIMITED
EDITORIAL
Managing Editor: Judy Poulos
Editorial Assistant: Ella Martin
Editorial Coordinator: Margaret Kelly

PHOTOGRAPHY
Steve Tanner, Di Lewis, Andrew Elton
Photographs on pages 53, 55 and 57 kindly
supplied by Jennifer Bennell

ILLUSTRATIONS
Margaret Metcalfe

DESIGN AND PRODUCTION
Manager: Sheridan Carter
Layout: Gavin Murrell
Finished Art: Steve Joseph

Contents

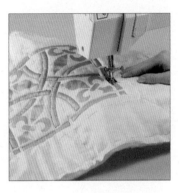

Painted Silk Scarf

Quilted Silk Pillows

Stenciled Curtain & Tie-back

Lacy Bed Linens

Sponged Draperies

Mediterranean Platter

Sophisticated Glasses

Painted Plates

Super Scales

Strawberry Tray

Folk Art Shelf

Transform your home with these decorative painting and stenciling projects for every room.

DECORATIVE PAINTING

Somewhere deep inside all of us is an artist just waiting for the opportunity to shine. In the past this has remained an unrealized ambition for most people. These days, thanks to the arrival of easy-to-use, almost foolproof, paints and the revival of traditional decorative techniques, anyone can be an artist.

Just as exciting is the discovery that you can use an enormous variety of objects and surfaces for your canvas. You can transform just about anything with some paint and a little imagination. Craft stores sell an increasing variety of objects specifically for this purpose, such as lidded chipwood boxes, plain china, paper lampshades, picture frames, and wood items of various kinds. If you are unsure of where to find these items, check the advertisements in your favorite craft magazine. Remember, too, that decorative painting techniques will do wonders for that much-used treasure stored in the garage.

In this book, you will find a host of easy-to-do projects that cover painting on glass, fabric, plaster, wood and ceramics. The full-sized templates for the designs are on the pattern sheet, ready for you to trace. You don't need to have any special skills – if you can trace a design and hold a paintbrush, you can achieve anything in this book.

CHOOSING YOUR DESIGN

If you are a novice, you will probably feel more comfortable using a template exactly as it is given. As you gain confidence and skill, experiment with the designs, changing elements or colors until you find an arrangement that pleases you. Sources of inspiration are all around you. As well as books, look out for tile and fabric patterns, china designs, gift-wrapping paper, ceramic tiles and wallpaper patterns.

Once you have chosen your design, you may find that it is not the size you need. The simplest way to enlarge or reduce a design is with a photocopier. If this is not possible, you will need to use the grid method which is described on page 7.

TRANSFERRING THE DESIGN

Some designs can be transferred quite easily to the object you are painting – particularly so when an irregular, freehand look is called for or if the design is very simple.

If you have a more complex design where some exactness is required, there is a method to help you. First, trace the design from the pattern sheet onto a piece of tracing paper. Next, place the tracing over the area it is to occupy and tape it in place with masking tape. Slip a piece of graphite paper (similar to carbon paper) between the tracing and the surface and go over the lines with a sharp pencil or dry ball-point pen. This will transfer the outline to the surface with lines of graphite which you can erase when the painting is complete. These graphite papers come in a light and a dark form so you can choose one that is appropriate to the surface on which you are painting.

MATERIALS

These days there is an enormous variety of paint and paint-type products on the market. For best results, you should always choose a product that is specifically formulated for the surface you are working on. Some products are multi-purpose and are therefore particularly useful to have in your collection.

Always try to buy the best brushes you can afford and look after them. Clean your brushes after every use – in paint thinner (mineral spirits) or water (for water-based paints). For more tips on looking after your brushes, see page 9.

You will need a variety of paintbrush sizes, from narrow liner brushes to quite large flat brushes, depending on the projects you choose. Begin with the brushes you need for your first project, then add to your collection as you go.

CHOOSING PAINTS
Acrylic Paints

The easiest paints to use, acrylic paints are available in a huge range of colors and sizes of containers (from tubes to large cans). Because they are water-based, clean-up is simple. Take care to attend to this quickly, because once the paint has dried, it will be as permanent as any solvent-based paint and will certainly ruin your brushes.

Acrylic paints can be applied to almost any surface and do not need primer or undercoat. They are equally suitable for indoor or outdoor use and are fully water-proof when dry.

Ceramic Paints

Ceramic paints should be used for items which are largely decorative. Available in a wide range of colors, they give a shiny finish to ceramics, glass, metal and even wood.

Above: Tiles, wrapping paper, fabric, books and china can all provide a rich source of painting designs

They can be coated with a ceramic varnish to give an even glossier and somewhat more durable surface. Do not put items painted with these paints in the dishwasher; wash them carefully by hand in warm soapy water.

Fabric Paints

There are a number of types of fabric paints available today and most are easy to apply. Read the manufacturer's information on the tube, jar or pen to find the one that is suitable for your purpose. Most fabric paints work best when applied to a white or cream surface but some will color a darker surface quite well. The range of colors is excellent and includes metallic shades as well.

Fabric pens are a very easy option if you want a little more control of the color, such as outlining or writing. Take care to tape your fabric down when using pens or straight-from-the-tube paints as the fabric can become wrinkled, making it difficult for you to work.

When considering fabric painting, check out the "puff" type paints and dimensional paints as well; they can give unusual highlights to your work.

Painting on silk requires a slightly different technique. It is crucial to use a frame when painting silk, in order to hold the silk firm and to keep it off the work surface. Special frames are available for this purpose or you can make your own, and special silk pins are used for fastening the silk to the frame. Once the silk is stretched quite tightly in the frame, tape the tracing of your design under the silk and trace over all the outlines with gutta, a gum-like substance. The gutta acts as a barrier, preventing the paint from spreading to an area where it is not wanted. The silk paints (or dyes) flow onto the silk and will flow through any breaks in the gutta. Make sure the gutta lines are continuous and any outlines are closed. Leave the gutta to dry for at least an hour before you begin applying the paint.

Once the paints are dry, the fabrics should be heat-set to make the paint permanent. There are a number of ways you can do this, including steaming, pressing with a warm iron, using your hairdryer, chemical solutions and even microwaving. Follow the manufacturer's instructions and choose the right method for the paints you have used.

Glass Paints

Ideal for decorative items, glass paints give the lovely effect of stained glass. Either solvent- or water-based, they should be applied carefully with a soft clean brush and left to dry for at least a day in a dust-free place. Because the paints do not flow as easily as some others do, a little practice is required to master their use. To achieve a strong, deep color, you may need to apply two coats

Before you begin painting the glass, wash it in warm soapy water, rinse, then dry it thoroughly. To remove any dust or adhering particles, wipe the glass with ammonia and water.

You can use glass paints to decorate china and ceramics but they are not suitable for items which need to cope with a lot of wear and tear. Do not put painted glass in the dishwasher; wash it by hand in lukewarm soapy water.

Other Paints

In addition to these general groups of paint products, there are other products that are quite suitable, such as felt pens. These are very inexpensive and easy to use on a variety of surfaces, such as paper, wood and plaster.

Stenciling paints or crayons are formulated specially to use with stencil brushes in the dabbing or pouncing motion that is required for stenciling. (See page 9 for more on stenciling paints.)

Varnish

Once you have completed your painting, you will need to decide whether to add a coat of varnish and, if you do, whether it should be matt or glossy. The choices are up to you but, generally, a coat of varnish is helpful in giving an extra layer of protection. Make sure your paints are completely dry before you varnish and that the product you use is compatible with the paints and surface it is covering.

Left: Tracing a design off a piece of fabric
Above: Drawing a stencil design from a tracing, leaving "bridges" in place

STENCILING

Welcome to the world of stenciling – one of the simplest and most satisfying ways of decorating with paint. Anyone can be a skillful stencil artist, even without the usual talents we associate with the term "artist". This book is like a stencil supermarket for the enthusiast. We provide you with a number of wonderful stencil designs – all you have to do is trace them and then cut out your stencil, following the detailed instructions for making stencils on the following pages.

Stenciling is a means of transferring a design, usually a regularly repeating design, to a surface, by applying paint through holes that have been cut out for that purpose. In fact, anything with holes in it, like a piece of lace or a doily, can function as a stencil.

The paints that are used are naturally dictated by the surface to be stenciled. The surface can be made of just about anything – plaster, fabric, wood, china, paper and more.

While stenciling is a very traditional means of decorating, the technique works just as well in a modern setting where it can add considerable warmth and character to an otherwise fairly sterile room*.

The process is not difficult to master. First decide on the motif for your stencil design. Look around and you will find you are surrounded by potential stencil designs – on your favorite china cup, the material of a dress, a book, or a wallpaper pattern. You could even design your own pattern for a stencil. Many people simplify matters even further with a pre-cut, ready-to-use stencil. These are becoming more and more popular and are available at quite reasonable cost from craft stores.

Using a popular stencil does not mean that your work will look the same as that of someone else who has used the same stencil. Everyone adds their own unique mark, in the colors they choose, the way in which they apply the paint and where they place the stencil.

You can stencil just about anything, but if you are a beginner, choose something small for your first project. Finishing that, and basking in the admiration of family and friends, will encourage you to continue, and to become more adventurous with each project.

See a stenciled room on page 62

HOW TO STENCIL

Tracing the Design

First choose your stencil design. This can be a motif from a book, a piece of fabric or wallpaper, gift-wrapping paper, or your own imagination.

If the design needs to be reduced or enlarged, the simplest method is to use a photocopier. If you do not have access to a photocopier, you will have to use the grid method. To do this, draw up a squared grid over the design. Draw another grid with the same number of squares on a fresh sheet of paper. If you want to enlarge the design, make these squares larger than those in the first grid. For example, if you want to double the size of the design, make the squares on the second grid twice the size of the first one. If you want to reduce the size, make the second grid smaller. Now, draw into each square of the second grid the contents of that square on the first grid, matching the points where outlines cross the grid lines. Don't try to draw in the details until all the main outlines are drawn. Continue in this way until you have transferred the entire design to the new grid.

Making the Stencil

If the design is to be used just as it is, with no changes to size or elements of the design, and if you are using clear acetate for your stencil, then it can be traced straight onto the acetate. To make a stencil, trace in the outlines of the elements adding small "bridges" so that color areas are enclosed by a continuous line.

For a multi-colored design, you will find it easier to work if you make a separate stencil for each color. Trace the entire design onto each stencil, using solid lines for all the parts in one color and dotted lines for the other outlines. These dotted lines will serve as registration marks for matching up the stencils. For a repeating design, such as a wall pattern or border, add some registration marks, or the dotted outline of the next element at the edges of the design, as well.

Cut out the areas of the design that are to be painted with a sharp craft knife. A cutting mat will hold the stencil material in place while you work. To ensure accurate cutting, use only the tip of the knife, moving it towards you. Begin cutting in the center of a space and work towards the edges, turning the acetate rather than the knife to cut around curves.

Painting the Stencil

Mark with a pencil any guidelines on the surface to be stenciled, such as the true vertical or the distance from a given edge. If the stencil is a repeating design, such as a border, mark in the position of each repeat of the design so that you can make any adjustments to the spacing.

To ensure a clean outline, the stencil must sit flush with the surface to be painted and be held there firmly. Tape the first stencil at its first position with low-tack masking tape.

Choose a paint that is appropriate to the surface to be stenciled. Pour a little of the paint into an old plate or dish – stenciling works best when the paint is used quite sparingly. Dip only the ends of the bristles of the stencil brush in the paint, then wipe off any excess paint on a piece of paper towel.

Apply small amounts of paint with a dabbing or pouncing motion. Make sure that you use enough paint to make a clear outline at the edges, but vary the depth of paint across the stencil to give an interestingly shaded effect. Don't use the paint too thickly.

The best fabric for stenciling is a close-woven natural one, such as cotton or silk. Wash and iron the fabric before pinning it on a work surface that has been protected with sheets of absorbent paper.

When you have large areas to cover and are looking for a soft mottled effect, stencil with a sponge. Always dampen the sponge first before picking up a little paint from the palette. Remove any excess paint on paper towels before you apply the paint with a light dabbing motion.

Clean your equipment with either water or a solvent, depending on the type of paint you have used. It is also very important to clean your stencil often as you work – paint build-up can distort the outlines and even block small holes.

MATERIALS

Tracing Paper and Pencil

Ideally, you will be able to trace your stencil design onto the actual stencil material, but there will be occasions when an intermediate step is required and it is then that you will need tracing paper and pencil. If you are going to adjust the design or isolate a part of it, you should trace it first onto tracing paper, then make whatever changes you wish before making your stencil.

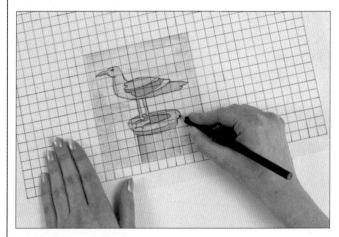

To enlarge a motif, first trace it onto a grid

The Stencil

For a long time, stencils have been made using thick manila cardboard coated with a 1:1 mixture of paint thinner and boiled linseed oil. The treated sheets are hung to dry and the excess coating carefully wiped off before use. The sheets are inexpensive and easy to work with, but they have the disadvantage of being opaque so you can't match up design elements or "see where you are going".

These days, clear plastic or acetate on rolls or sheets is often used for making stencils instead of manila cardboard. Choose an acetate that is thick enough to stand up to the wear and tear but not so thick that it is difficult to cut. Because these materials are transparent, they eliminate the need for tracing the design onto tracing paper and then transferring it to the stencil material. You can trace the design directly onto the acetate with a fine felt-tip permanent marker.

Sharp Craft Knife

Once the design is traced onto the acetate, you will need to cut out those areas that will be covered by paint. Scissors are not suitable; you will need a sharp craft knife.

Cutting Mat

A rubber mat for cutting on is quite useful but not essential. If you will be using one frequently, it is probably quite a good investment, as the rubber surface not only protects your work surface but your blades as well. The mats are printed with grid lines which are useful for drawing and cutting straight lines.

Masking Tape

A roll of masking tape in two or three widths is a must for stenciling. You will need tape for holding tracings in place, for securing stencils, and for masking surfaces that you wish to protect from paint. The tape is also very useful for making repairs to torn or damaged stencils – much easier than making a new one.

It is possible to buy low-tack masking tape which can be removed without damaging the painted surface. Whether you use low-tack masking tape or the ordinary variety, always exercise great care when pulling the tape away from the surface.

Stencil Brushes

Stenciling requires special brushes that are quite different from ordinary paintbrushes in that the bristle end is flat rather than pointed. This shape is dictated by the way in which stencils are painted – with a dabbing or "pouncing" motion rather than by stroking.

Always choose the best brushes you can afford and look after them well. Clean them after every use (either in water or solvent – depending on the paint used). If you clean them in solvent, wash them afterwards in a mild detergent solution and dry the bristles with paper towels. Never leave paint on the brushes and never store them soaking in water or solvent. Once they are clean and dry, store them standing, with bristles up, in a jar or similar container.

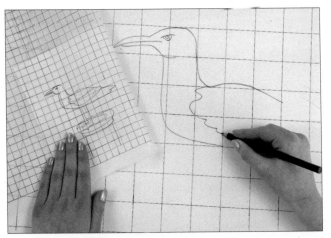

Enlarging the motif by copying it onto a larger grid

Sponges

Natural sponges are very useful for stenciling where the design is quite open and where a soft-textured appearance is desired. Clean your sponges in the same way as the brushes and, when dry, store them in a suitable container.

Paints

You can use just about any paint for stenciling; your choice will usually depend on the surface. There are paints available which are specially made for stenciling. They have the advantage of being fast-drying, allowing you to paint, remove the stencil and place it in its next position more quickly than you can with most other paints. Stencil paints come in a wide range of colors and can also be mixed to create any color you wish.

For stenciling on fabric, you can choose from a wide range of paint. Some have the consistency of a thick liquid, others are in powder form, and others are applied directly from a bottle. To allow the item to be washed, the paint needs to be made permanent by fixing with heat. Follow the manufacturer's instructions to heat-set the particular paint you have used.

Special ceramic paints are available for use on tiles, china, ornaments, and glass. While these paints are technically permanent, you will need to treat the stenciled object with a little care.

Many other paints can be used for stenciling, including ordinary house paints (either water- or oil-based). Cans of spray paint, made for motor vehicles, are very simple to use where a quick overall effect is required on walls, metal surfaces or plastics. If you do choose spray paints, take extra care to mask off the surrounding area with drop-cloths or newspaper before you begin; the spray can travel a surprising distance.

Artists' acrylic colors make great stencil paints, particularly for surfaces which need to be flexible.

Ruler

A long plastic ruler is very useful to mark straight lines for placement of the design, or for drawing in registration marks for matching up stencils.

WALL FINISHES

If you are working on old walls – or new ones for that matter – great care must be given to the preparation. As with so many aspects of interior decoration, the better the preparation, the better the final result.

Before starting to paint the walls, spend some time practicing on sample boards so that you get the feel of creating the paint finish. If you have a wall or two on which to practice, such as a small bathroom or laundry area (they can always be repainted!), try the finish on those walls before embarking on a more ambitious project.

You can now start painting the walls with eggshell finish enamel. (The color is up to you, but generally a room or a whole house can happily be prepared in white eggshell finish enamel and then any color or colors imposed over the white.) If you cannot buy eggshell paint, you can easily make it yourself by mixing one part matt/flat enamel with one part satin enamel, creating the slight sheen seen on eggshells.

If you do not wish to work in oil-based paints, you can make the same eggshell finish using latex acrylic house paints. However, a word of warning: when applying a decorative paint glaze to walls, the glaze is more workable and stays "open" (does not dry out immediately) longer if it is imposed on an oil-based paint rather than on an acrylic paint. Acrylic paints are very absorbent and tend to soak up a decorative paint glaze in a very thirsty manner and make it much more difficult to work.

You can use a brush or a roller to apply the paint. Rollers are very quick, but tend to leave behind the appearance of an orange skin. To overcome this orange-peel effect, lay on one section with the roller – about 24 ins at a time, then quickly come back over the wet paint with a good bristle brush and "lay off", that is, pull the brush from the ceiling down to the baseboard through the paint, removing the orange-peel pattern in the paint. If you do this carefully, the paint surface should be absolutely smooth.

Doors, moldings, baseboards and windows should be prepared in the same way, using a brush to apply the paint. After the application of two coats of eggshell finish enamel the walls may look opaque. If this is the case, you are then ready to get on with the decorative glaze. If, however, there are patches on the wall which have a slightly gray appearance, you must apply more coats of eggshell finish paint until the wall is absolutely opaque.

Once the walls are a solid color, they are ready to receive the decorative glaze. If, in spite of all your hard work, you have not been able to achieve an absolutely even, smooth surface, there are some glazes which will not be suitable. For instance, the dragged finish requires a very smooth, even surface, allowing the brush to glide over the wall without meeting any bumps.

MASKING

Before applying the decorative glaze you must mask baseboards, moldings, windows and doors if you are to achieve a first-class, professional finish. Use a low-tack tape, which is half low-tack and the other half brown paper. The half that is brown paper will provide extra protection to the masked areas. Be careful at the corners where it does not bond well to itself; you will need a length of ordinary tape over the top to make sure the bonding is secure at that point.

Taking the trouble to mask off areas properly is well worth the effort. Your finish will be crisp and clean on all the edges and you will have no cleaning up to do. Ignore this step and you will spend many tedious hours removing unwanted paint.

TOOLS AND SUPPLIES

To achieve the best results, good tools and supplies are of the utmost importance. Buy them as you need them, beginning with the basics and adding to them as necessary.

◇ *eggshell enamel (one part matt/flat enamel to one part satin enamel or one part matt/flat latex acrylic to one part satin acrylic)*
◇ *matt/flat enamel paints*
◇ *water-based artists' acrylic colors*
◇ *universal tints*
◇ *oil-based and water-based scumble medium*
◇ *paint thinner*
◇ *shellac*

- ❖ *rollers*
- ❖ *denatured alcohol*
- ❖ *roller covers*
- ❖ *roller pans (trays)*
- ❖ *wall stipple brush (rectangular)*
- ❖ *cutting-in (detail) brush, 2"*
- ❖ *2"-3" paintbrushes*
- ❖ *dragging brush*
- ❖ *round stipple brush*
- ❖ *natural sponges*
- ❖ *muslin (cut and washed) – buy new muslin, cut in 22 yd lengths, then wash it and put it through the dryer to remove lint before cutting it into short lengths*
- ❖ *container for mixing*
- ❖ *large stirring sticks*
- ❖ *strainer bags (nylon pantyhose are ideal)*
- ❖ *duster brush*
- ❖ *tack cloths*
- ❖ *lint-free dust cloths*
- ❖ *masking tape and tape dispenser*
- ❖ *razor blades*
- ❖ *ladders*

GLAZE

Antiquing glaze is a semi-translucent medium composed of linseed oil, turpentine or paint thinner, whiting and extenders.

Glazing is essential. It adds translucency to the paint, extends the drying time – which means you have more time to work with the paint once it has been applied and enables the paint to hold the imprint of the tool. If you did not use glaze and performed, say, a sponged finish, you would find the paint had closed up into an opaque color within an hour or two.

Oil-based and water-based glazes have the same characteristics, although they are obviously made from entirely different materials.

CLEANING TOOLS

Most painting tools used for oil-based paints can be cleaned first by soaking in paint thinner, then by washing in hot, soapy water. If using water-based paints, washing the brushes in hot soapy water then rinsing them in clear water will do the trick. Rinse thoroughly – tools will harden and become useless if any paint residue is left after washing.

All brushes must be carefully rinsed after use. Have two or three tins of paint thinner ready to use.

To soften a hardened brush, dip it into a saucepan of boiling water, detergent and ammonia – or immerse in paint stripper or brush cleaner for a short time.

PREPARATION

Preparation is crucial to a successful result. All walls should be sanded back and, where necessary, filled.

Once the filler is dry and sanded, so that the filling is imperceptible, the filled area must be sealed. If you do not seal the filled area, you will find it shows through as a gray patch when you apply the wall glaze.

Shellac is a sealing medium. It is thinned with denatured alcohol and dries almost immediately, so that you can get on with the painting job immediately. If shellac is not available, use whatever sealer you can buy at your local suppliers. It is most important that the walls are well sanded and made as smooth as you can possibly make them.

Once the wall is in as good a condition as you can possibly achieve and all sanding has been completed, wipe it down with muslin rags and vacuum the floor and walls. Then wipe the whole wall with tack cloths. These are made of cheesecloth, impregnated with linseed oil, and are invaluable for removing dust.

Fabric Painting

Painting on fabric is not a modern fad – it has been known since ancient times. These days, with the variety of paints and fabrics available, the possibilities for fabric painting are limitless. Painting your own fabric is a wonderful way of stamping your individuality on your surroundings.

The most common way to use fabric painting is to decorate a piece of fabric, which is then made up in the usual way into a garment or soft decorative accent. The other method is to take an existing garment or home accessory and then paint a design or motif on it.

Choose paints that are suitable to the project you have in mind, taking into account such factors as wearability and washability. Most fabric paints must be set or "fixed" with heat to make them permanent and washable.

The delightful tea cloth opposite has been stenciled in a design that mirrors the china pattern. To make a cloth like this, isolate an element or two of your favorite china pattern. It need not be an exact copy but should be harmonious and the colors should match as closely as possible. In this case, separate stencils were made for the border pattern and the corner motif. These were then stenciled around the cloth and napkins as shown. When the paint was dry, the cloth and napkins were pressed on the wrong side with a hot iron to fix the paints, following the manufacturer's instructions.

When you are planning your cloth, take note of which parts of the cloth will be visible when it is laid on the table. Don't waste your efforts on those parts which will not be seen.

PAINTED SILK SCARF

Silk painting, which is much easier than it looks, is not only a very satisfying hobby but also a wonderful source of presents for friends and family.

Left: Tracing the design
Above: The completed scarf

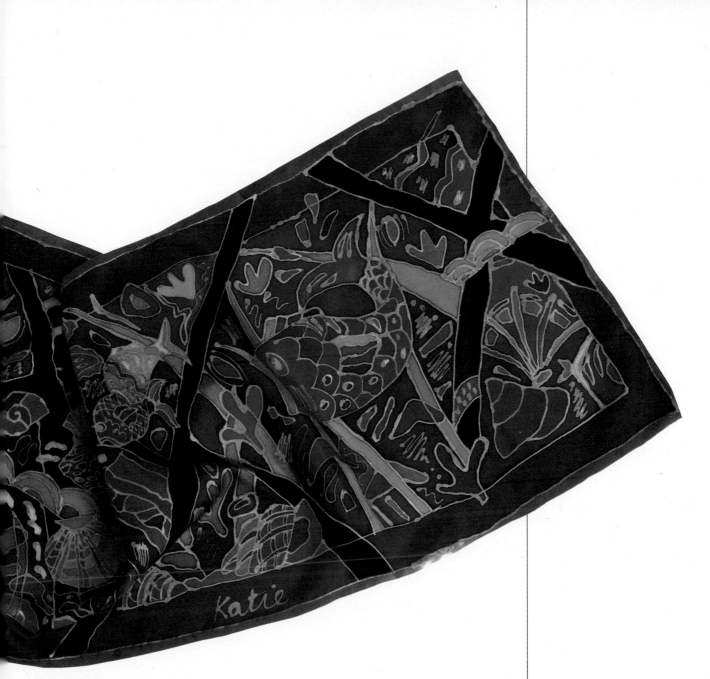

MATERIALS

tracing paper and pencil
36" square or 12" x 48" of
*   plain silk (Habutai no. 8)*
silk frame
silk pins
masking tape
clear gutta
silk paints
soft paintbrush

INSTRUCTIONS

See the design on the Pull Out
Pattern Sheet.

1 Enlarge the design from the
Pattern Sheet to the required size to
cover your piece of silk. If you do not
have access to a photocopier to enlarge
the design, use the grid method (see
page 7).

2 Stretch the length of silk over the
frame, using special silk pins.
Frames suitable for this purpose are
available from craft stores, ready for you
to assemble. A frame is essential for silk
painting as it keeps the silk quite taut
and raised off the work surface.

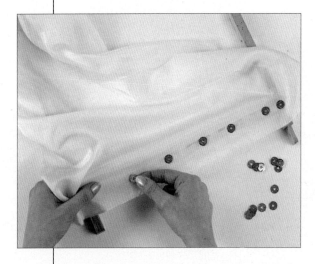

3 Tape the design to the frame underneath the silk so that you can see it clearly through the fabric. Trace in the main outlines with the pencil.

4 Follow the pencil lines with the gutta (a gum-like material which serves to separate areas of color, preventing one color from bleeding into another). For the gutta to be effective the lines must be continuous; any gaps will allow the silk paint to seep through. Allow the gutta to dry for an hour before beginning to paint.

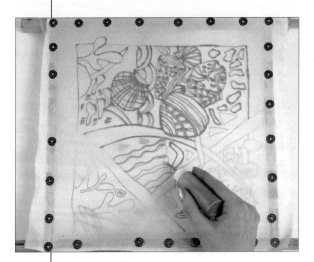

5 Apply the paints with a soft brush, applying the color between the lines of gutta and letting the paint creep up to the lines. Clean the brush in water before dipping it in the next color.

6 When the painting is complete and the paint is dry, you can fix the colors by one of the following methods: iron on the back of the silk, steam the silk in a pressure cooker or professional steamer, or use a combination of microwave and fixative. Be guided by the instructions on the paint bottles. Your scarf is now ready to hem.

Top left: Pinning the silk to the frame
Center left: Outlining the design with the gutta
Left: Painting the design

*Quilted silk pillows
(see page 18)*

QUILTED SILK PILLOWS

*These elegant
cream silk
pillows have
been stenciled
with metallic
fabric paints and
then quilted for a
really luxurious
effect.*

MATERIALS
*18" square of cream silk for the
   pillow front*
*2 pieces of cream silk, each
   10" x 18", for the pillow
   back*
brown paper
masking tape
sheets of clear acetate for the stencils
sharp craft knife
cutting board (optional)
fine felt-tip permanent marker
stencil brush
metallic fabric paints
old dish or plate for a palette
18" square of polyester batting
cream sewing thread
10" zipper
12" pillow form

INSTRUCTIONS
See the design on the Pull Out Pattern
Sheet.
1/2" seam allowances are included.

1 Fold the silk square into halves
   and then into quarters. Press in
the creases.

2 Trace the stencil design from the
   Pattern Sheet onto the acetate
with the fine felt-tip marker, marking in
the horizontal and vertical lines on the
design. These indicate the center of the
complete design.

3 Cut out the areas to be painted
   with the craft knife.

4 Tape the silk square on the
   work surface (which has been
protected with layers of brown
paper). Position the stencil on the
silk square, matching the pressed
lines with the drawn lines on the
stencil. Tape the stencil in place on
the silk square.

5 Pour a small amount of the
   metallic fabric paint into the dish
or plate. Load the stencil brush with a
small amount of paint and, with a
dabbing motion, begin to color in the
stencil. Allow the paint to dry before
lifting the stencil.

6 Reposition the stencil around the
   silk square, each time lining up
the lines with the creases and allowing
the paint to dry before moving on to
the next position. When all the painting is complete, leave to dry for
twenty-four hours, then set the paint
with a medium-to-hot iron.

7 Baste the square of polyester
   batting to the wrong side of the
painted silk square. Use several rows of
basting to ensure the layers are held
together securely.

8 Machine-quilt around some of the motifs or around all of them if you prefer.

9 Place the pillow backs with right sides together. Join them along one side with a 4"-long seam at each end, leaving the middle merely basted for the zipper. Press the seam open. Sew in the zipper and leave it open.

10 Place the pillow back and front together with right sides facing. Sew around the outside, $^1/_2$" from edges of front. Trim the seams and turn the pillow to the right side through the zipper opening. Press lightly.

11 Stitch parallel rows around the cushion cover, stitching through all layers to make a $2^1/_2$" border all round.

12 Place the pillow form inside the stenciled cover.

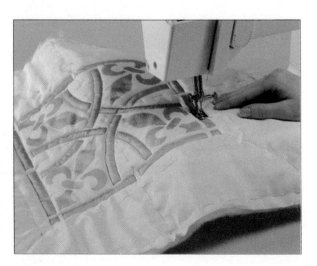

Far left: Lining up the stencil on the silk square
Above: Painting in the stencil design
Left: Quilting around the stenciled motifs

STENCILED CURTAIN & TIE-BACK

A simple muslin curtain takes on a new elegance with a padded and stenciled border and matching tie-back. The instructions given here are for making the border only. You will need to make up your own curtain when the border is attached.

Below: Painting in the stencil curtain design
Below right: Pinning the stenciled fabric over the interfacing
Far right: The completed curtain and tie-back

MATERIALS
sufficient muslin fabric
masking tape
firm interfacing (non-fusible)
tracing paper
pencil
sheets of clear acetate for the stencils
fine felt-tip permanent marker
sharp craft knife
newspaper
brown paper
fabric paint
old dish or plate for a palette
stencil brush
piping (either ready-made or make your own)
pelmet stiffening or very firm fusible interfacing
pins
matching sewing thread
2 small brass rings

INSTRUCTIONS
See the design on the Pull Out Pattern Sheet.
$1/2$" seam allowances are included.

CURTAIN BORDER

1 Cut a piece of muslin 10" wide and the length of the curtain. You will probably need to cut this down the length of the fabric so as to avoid any seams.

2 Trace the stencil design from the Pattern Sheet on the acetate using the felt-tip marker. Cut out the stencil with the sharp knife.

3 Cover your work surface with newspaper with a sheet of brown paper on top. Tape the fabric strip to this work surface.

4 Position the stencil on one end of the strip, 2" from one long edge. Tape the stencil in place.

5 Pour a little of the fabric paint into the dish. Load the stencil brush with a small amount of the paint and paint in the stencil design with a dabbing motion. Leave this section to dry before lifting the stencil and placing it on the next section to be painted.

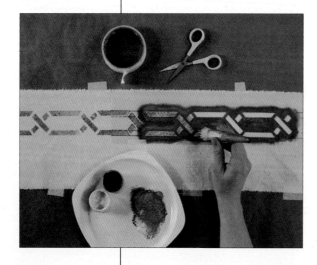

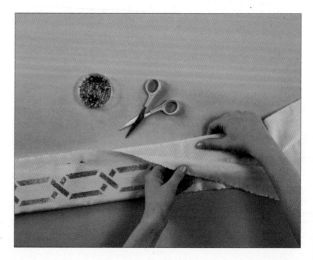

Right: Stenciling the tie-back
Below right: To attach the piping around the tie-back, clip the curves

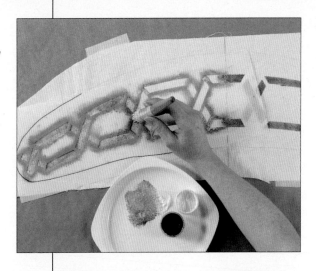

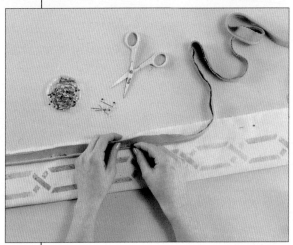

close to the piping. Press the unpainted half of the border over, folding the opposite long edge to the wrong side of the curtain. Turn under the raw edge and slipstitch in place. Press well.

TIE-BACK

See the design on the Pull Out Pattern Sheet.

1 Cut two pieces of muslin to the shape of the tie-back. Make the stencil in the same way as for the curtain border. Mark the outline of the tie-back and the halfway point.

2 Place one piece of fabric and paint the stencil in the same way as for the curtain border, lifting the stencil (when the paint is dry) to paint in the second half, matching the pattern and the halfway points.

3 Cut the pelmet stiffening to the same shape as the tie-back. Remove the backing and press it onto the back of the stenciled muslin. If using the fusible interfacing, ignore the reference to the backing.

4 Trim away the excess. Pin the piping to the stenciled front with right sides facing and raw edges even. Clip the curves for ease. Stitch around the edge, close to the piping cord.

5 Place stenciled front on the back, right sides facing. Sew along previous stitching line (for piping), leaving an opening for turning. Turn to the right side. Turn seam allowances to the inside and slipstitch the opening closed. Press well. Sew a small brass ring to each end.

When you reposition the stencil, take care to match the pattern exactly. Fix all the paint when it is dry.

6 Fold the fabric strip lengthwise in half, with wrong sides together, placing a double thickness of interfacing in between. Pin the top (painted) layer of the muslin and the interfacing together along the top edge.

7 Pin and stitch the piping to the top edge of the muslin and the interfacing only, with right sides together, and leaving the bottom layer of muslin unsewn.

8 Pin the piped edge to the edge of your curtain, with right sides facing and raw edges even. Stitch

Lacy bed linen (see page 24)

23

LACY BED LINENS

This is a delightful way to create the effect of exclusive lace-trimmed bed linens without the cost. All you need is a short length of lace which you can use to stencil the design onto pillowcases, sheets and duvet covers.

MATERIALS

plain sheet, pillowcase and duvet cover
length of lace, approximately 2¼" wide
narrow masking tape
newspaper
sheets of brown paper
pins
black fabric paint
water
mouth-spray diffuser
gray and peach satin ribbon, ³/₈" and ⁵/₈" wide
matching sewing thread

INSTRUCTIONS

1 Starting at one end of the wide hem at the top end of the sheet, pin the lace in place so that the decorative edge of the lace runs along the hemmed edge. Place a line of masking tape to cover the two short ends and the long straight edge of the lace.

2 Lay sheets of newspaper on your work surface to protect it from overspray. Lay brown paper on top of the newspaper to protect the bed linen from the dye in the newsprint.

3 Remove the pins from the lace and lay the section of sheet with the lace attached on the brown paper. Cover all parts of the sheet, except for the lace section, with more brown paper, taping it in place.

4 In a small bottle, mix the black fabric paint with sufficient water to give a thin, very liquid consistency. Test the effect on a piece of scrap fabric, using the mouth-spray diffuser. Aim for a light-gray spotty texture that will spread through the holes in the lace onto the fabric. When you are confident with the color and the diffuser, spray the lace-covered sheet in the same way. Leave to dry.

5 Move the length of lace along the sheet top, re-masking in the same way each time, until the whole length of the border is complete. Remove all the masking and leave the paint to dry for twenty-four hours.

6 Fix the paint using an iron set to the hottest setting appropriate for the sheet fabric.

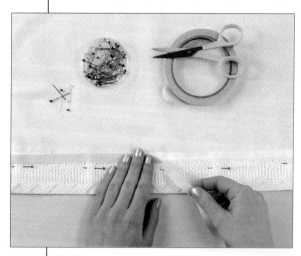

Top: Pinning and taping the lace in place
Right: Spraying the paint over the lace

24

7 Pin and stitch a length of $^3/_8$"-wide peach ribbon and $^5/_8$" gray ribbon parallel to the edge of the lace, turning in the raw edges at the ends.

8 To decorate the pillowcases and duvet cover, mask, pin and spray the lace in the same way up to the first corner. At the corner, stick masking tape across the lace at an angle of 45° to miter the corner. To continue along the next side, match up the pattern in the lace, mitering again at the corner with masking tape. Continue in this way until the border on all four sides is complete. Sew on peach satin ribbon as for the sheet.

Top: Pinning the lengths of ribbon in place
Above: Miter the corners on the pillowcases using masking tape

SPONGED DRAPERIES

These simple floor-length draperies will add style to any modern living room and can be painted in any color to complement your decor. The technique is so simple that even the children can paint a set of draperies for their own rooms.

MATERIALS
sufficient plain fabric
sheets of newspaper
masking tape
opaque black and white fabric
*   paints*
old dish or plate for a palette
natural sponge

INSTRUCTIONS

1 Mask all around your work area with plenty of newspaper before you begin.

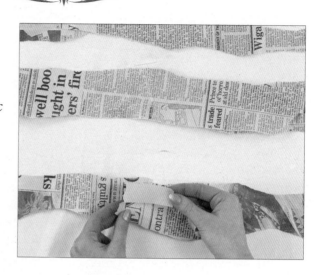

2 Tear sheets of newspaper into long irregularly shaped strips. Do not try to be too neat – the effect will be more dramatic if you allow a fair degree of variation.

3 Measure the area to be covered by the draperies. Your fabric will need to be twice the width of the window times the length to the floor, plus an allowance for hems and headings. Sew together enough fabric for your draperies but do not hem them or make the heading. Lay the fabric on newspaper spread over a large work area.

4 With masking tape, join together enough strips of newspaper to fit across the width of the fabric.

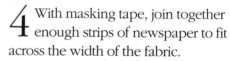

5 Leaving irregular gaps between the rows, stick the newspaper strips across the fabric, using little loops of masking tape to join the underside of the newspaper to the fabric. Cover the length of the fabric in this way, breaking up the rows with small "islands" of paper as you move towards the top.

6 Pour some black paint into the dish or plate. Dip the damp sponge into the paint and, starting at the bottom, apply the paint between the rows of newspaper.

7 At the beginning of each new row, add a little white paint to the black, adding more white paint with each successive row so that the color gradually lightens to gray as you work up the fabric. When you reach the top where you have the islands of paper, the color should be quite light.

8 Allow the paint to dry before removing the strips of newspaper. Make the other drapery in the same way.

9 When the paint is dry, iron each piece of fabric on the wrong side to fix the color. Finish making the draperies in the usual way.

Top left: Sticking irregularly shaped strips of newspaper across the fabric
Center left: Applying the paint with a sponge to the area between the paper strips
Bottom left: When the paint is dry, remove the strips of newspaper
Right: The completed draperies

Ornamental Painting

Painting your own designs on kitchenware, glassware and ornaments will give your home a style that is quite unique. You will be able to turn inexpensive crockery from the supermarket into pieces you will be proud to display.

There are special paints available for decorating glass, ceramics, china and wood. Choose the right paint for the job and carefully follow the manufacturer's instructions. While the special ceramic and glass paints are relatively easy to use and are designed for a purpose, they are not intended for items that will take a great deal of wear. Keep them for the more ornamental pieces.

More hardy are these painted terracotta pots which are definitely meant to be used. Paint the pots with simple designs of your own or isolate an element from any of the stencil designs given in this book. Stenciling a pot is quite simple as long as you take care to keep the stencil in contact with the pot and tape it in place while you work.

You can make a very simple but effective design by masking off areas of the pot with masking tape and then sponging the exposed areas. Experiment with combinations of colors and designs to build up a collection of personalized pots like this to dress up a sunny corner. Oil-based semi-gloss paints or artists' acrylic colors are both quite suitable for use on terracotta.

MEDITERRANEAN PLATTER

Bring all the sunshine of the Mediterranean into your home with this brightly colored platter. This method of decorating is called "resist painting" where a material (in this case the china marker) prevents the paint from covering a certain area. To create this primitive design, you will need a mixture of glass and ceramic paints.

MATERIALS
plain white platter
glass paint, emerald green
ceramic paints in 4 colors of
   your choice
paintbrushes for applying the design
   and a larger one for the varnish
china marker
soft dry cloth
paint thinner
ceramic varnish

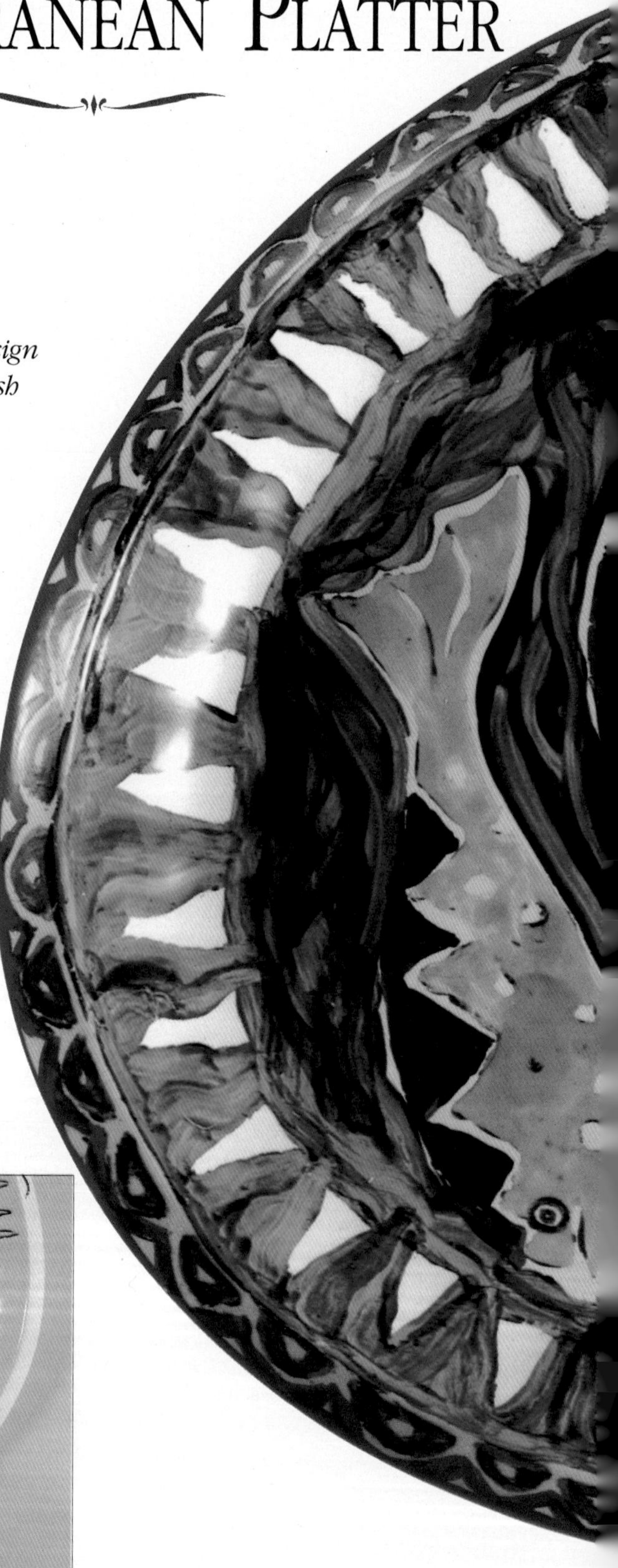

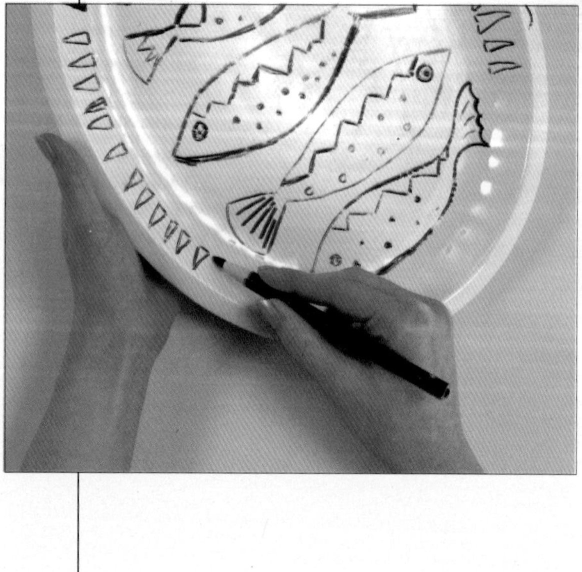

Right: Drawing the design with a chinagraph marker

*Above: The completed platter
Right: Painting the design with ceramic paints*

INSTRUCTIONS

1 Practice drawing the fish motif on a scrap of paper until you are happy with it, then, using the china marker, draw the design onto the platter. Those areas that are covered with the china marker will remain white on the finished platter.

2 Carefully paint in the fish with the ceramic paints. Keep the colors bright with a strong contrast such as deep blue and yellow, purple and orange, or black and gold.

3 Paint the border pattern in another pair of bright colors such as red and blue. Don't try to be too neat. This primitive style lends itself quite well to a little irregularity.

4 Paint the water around the fish in emerald green glass paint, applying the paint in a wave pattern to indicate water and waves. Use glass paint for this part of the design as it is more translucent than ceramic paint.

5 When the paint is completely dry, rub off the china marker lines with the soft dry cloth to reveal the white china beneath.

6 If you need to tidy up the edges of the platter, use the soft cloth soaked in paint thinner.

7 To protect your platter, paint it with a coat of ceramic varnish.

Above: Cleaning off the china marker
Right: Applying a coat of ceramic varnish

SOPHISTICATED GLASSES

MATERIALS
scrap paper
pencil
wine glasses
glass paint in the colors of
    your choice
fine paintbrush

INSTRUCTIONS

1 Before you begin painting, it is a good idea to plan your design on some scrap paper. Don't be too restricted by this plan; just use it to decide what works well and what doesn't.

2 Using the fine paintbrush, begin working from either the top or the bottom of the glass, painting a winding vine around the bowl and stem. To ensure that the paint does not smudge while you are working, allow one area to dry before beginning the next one.

Above right: The completed glasses
Below left and right: Painting in the design of the vines and leaves

Painted Plates

What a very bright and happy image these clowns create when painted on a set of wall plaques! They make the perfect decoration for a child's room. Birthday cards, gift-wrap, toys and children's picture books are all good sources of inspiration for a project like this one.

MATERIALS
white ceramic plates
tracing paper
pencil
china marker
ceramic paints: black, cherry red, lavender, blue, orange, yellow and green
ceramic varnish

INSTRUCTIONS

1 Draw or trace your chosen design on tracing paper, then copy it onto a plate using the china marker.

2 Take into account the round shape of the plate when you are drawing your design. You can make the feet follow the edge or the hands appear to support the top edge, or

have the clown doing a handstand. Whatever design you choose, always cover as much of the plate as possible.

3 Draw in the outline with a line of black ceramic paint, then paint in the main features, such as the clothes and hair. Color the clothes very bright and busy, with plenty of spots, checks and patches.

4 Fill in the background with another busy pattern of circles, triangles or wavy lines painted in more bright contrasting colors.

5 Allow the paint to dry completely, then paint with a protective coat of ceramic varnish.

Sketching the design from a greeting card

Drawing the design onto the plate

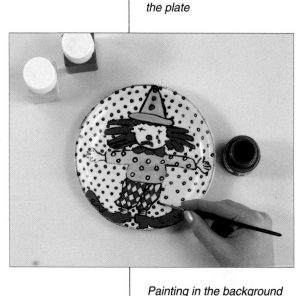

Painting in the background
Left: The completed plates

35

SUPER SCALES

A set of old scales becomes a stylish decorator item when it is painted in gold and black with a traditional design highlighted in old gold.

MATERIALS
scrap paper
pencil
old kitchen scales
fine sandpaper
ceramic paints: gold and black
gold spray paint
1" paintbrush
fine paintbrush
newspaper

INSTRUCTIONS

1 Clean the scales thoroughly with soapy water to remove all the grease and grime, then sand down with the fine sandpaper.

2 Apply one coat of black paint with the 1" brush. Apply a second coat, if required, to completely cover the old finish. Leave to dry.

3 Choose an appropriate design from a book, a stencil design, wallpaper or fabric. Experiment with the design on paper until you are happy with the result.

4 Using the fine brush, paint the outline of the design in gold, then fill it in with more gold paint.

5 If the scales are to be ornamental only, spray the dish of the scales with gold paint. If you are going to use the scales for weighing food, it is better not to paint the dish, but to clean it up with a good metal scourer. Always use spray paints in a well-ventilated area and mask the surrounding area carefully with newspaper to protect it from any overspray.

Above: The completed scales
Right: Paint the scales with black ceramic paint
Far right: Paint in the design with gold ceramic paint

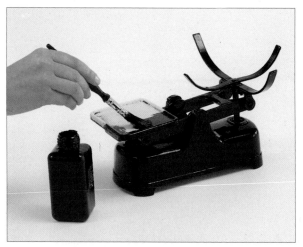

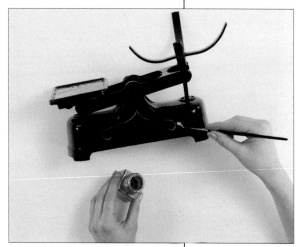

STRAWBERRY TRAY

What a charming notion! Decorate a simple pine tray with a pattern derived from your favorite china tea set. On the other hand, if you like this strawberry design, you can buy some china to match. Or you can use the techniques described here to paint a tray to match your own tea set.

Top: Tracing the design from the tea set
Above: Cutting out the stencil

MATERIALS
pine tray
tracing paper
pencil
masking tape
sheets of clear acetate for the stencils
colored pencils in appropriate colors
fine felt-tip permanent marker
sharp craft knife
cutting board (optional)
sandpaper
lint-free cloth
acrylic paints in appropriate colors
    (quick-drying stencil paints are
    ideal)
small stencil brush
old dish or plate for a palette
clear varnish
2" paintbrush

INSTRUCTIONS

1 Tape small pieces of tracing paper over the areas of the design you wish to use. Trace off the elements either singly, as single leaves and strawberries, or as groups.

2 Using your tracings, combine the elements into a pleasing design. Trace the new outline on another sheet of tracing paper. It is a good idea at this stage to color in your design with the colored pencils so you can judge its effectiveness.

3 Transfer the design to several sheets of acetate (one for each color), using the felt-tip marker.

4 You will need to make a separate stencil for each color. To do this, cut out of each sheet the elements you wish to paint in a particular color, using the craft knife. Take care when

cutting out to leave "bridges" in the design such as down the spine of a leaf or between stalks and leaves.

5 Sand the tray all over with the sandpaper until it is quite smooth. Wipe away the sandings with the lint-free cloth.

6 Position the first stencil (in this case the green one) on a corner of the tray and tape it in place. Place a small amount of paint in the dish or plate. Using the small stencil brush, paint in the green areas of the design using a dabbing motion. Take care not to load the brush with too much paint. Repeat the process for all the green areas on the tray. Allow the paint to dry completely.

7 With the clean stencil brush, paint in the next color (red) in the same way as the green, then the white and finally the yellow. To avoid smudging, make sure each last color is dry before you apply the next one.

8 To complete the tray, you can decorate around the sides and around the handles with small stencils.

9 When all the stenciling is complete and the paint is dry, apply a coat of clear varnish to all the surfaces.

Below: Painting the first color
Bottom: Completing the painting of the stencil

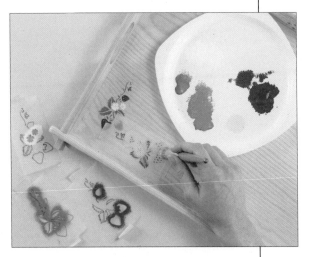

FOLK ART SHELF

This delightful little shelf, destined to house a collection of thimbles, has been painted with a number of traditional folk art motifs relating to sewing and quilting. Craft stores and unfinished wood furniture outlets sell similar shelves, or you could ask any amateur carpenter to build one for you.

MATERIALS
small wood shelf
fine felt-tip permanent marker
blue transfer paper
stylus
kneadable eraser
lint-free cloth
round sable brush, size 2
flat brushes, sizes 4 and 6
pale cream and dusty blue paint for base coats
folk art paints, suitable for painting on wood: gray blue, white, navy blue, cranberry, burnt umber, avocado green, black, light blue, raw sienna, light brown, rose, lavender, light gray, dark gray
spray gloss varnish
wet and dry sandpaper, 600 grade
normal sandpaper

INSTRUCTIONS
See the designs on the Pull Out Pattern Sheet.

PREPARATION
1 Paint the shelf with four base coats of pale cream, sanding well between each coat. Do not sand the final coat.

2 Trace the painting designs and transfer them to the positions shown on the shelf, using the stylus and transfer paper. Blue transfer paper is not as waxy as graphite paper and will not clog the nib of your pen as you draw over the design lines.

3 Outline all the tracing lines using the felt-tip marker. If you make a mistake, wet a small piece of the wet and dry sandpaper and gently rub the mistake away.

4 Let the ink dry for about one hour, then remove all visible lines with the kneadable eraser.

PAINTING
1 Paint this shelf in washes, i.e. a mix of 80% water and 20% paint. Use the round brush, size 2, for this step. When all the washes are finished, shade with the flat brush that fits best in the area you are shading. Shading is done with full-strength paint and only the water in your brush.

2 Mix French gray blue and snow white. Wash all hearts, dots and commas dividing each drawing, the ribbon on one bonnet, the scissor handles, the fabric on the quilt, the ruching on the dress, the band on the dress collar, two buttons, the bow on the straw hat, two pin heads, the bottom half of the fan, and the lettering. Shade in uniform blue.

3 Mix cranberry wine and burnt umber. Wash the button, all the flowers, stripes on the large button, and the quilt fabric. Shade with the same mixture.

4 Mix avocado, ebony black and snow white. Wash all the leaves and quilt fabric. Shade with a mixture of avocado and blue haze.

5 With blue haze, wash the handbag and the feather on the pen. Shade with blue haze.

6 With raw sienna, wash the letter next to the pen, the straw hat, the

Annette Johnson

pin box, the button, the ruler, the thimble, the calendar, the quilt fabric, the nib of the pen, and the ink label. Shade with light cinnamon.

7 With light cinnamon, wash the pen handle, the umbrella handle, the cotton spool ends, the boot heel and sole. Shade with burnt umber.

8 With dusty rose, wash the umbrella frills, the top section of the fan, the button, the quilt, the scallop part of the boot, the bow on the handbag. Shade with burnt umber.

9 Mix lavender and neutral gray. Wash the cotton on the spool, the quilt, a button, the bow on the fan, the pins, the umbrella and bows, the quilt edge. Shade with the same mix.

10 With uniform blue, wash the ink bottle and the back part of the boot. Shade with uniform blue.

11 With snow white, wash the dress and bonnet. Shade with slate gray. With slate gray, wash the scissor blades. Shade with ebony black. When all the painting is dry, reinforce with the felt-tip marker any lines painted over. Paint the shelf edges with a 1:1 mixture of cream and dusty blue.

12 Varnish the shelf all over when the paint is dry.

If you wish, give your shelf an antique finish with burnt umber oil paint or antiquing liquid before varnishing.

Furniture Facelifts

Decorative painting can work miracles on furniture that has become a little "tired" and worn. Whether you have an attic, basement or garage full of well-used chairs or are a devotee of tag sales, consider the possibilities that painting opens up.

Before you begin, make sure that the piece of furniture is worth all your hard work. Check that the structure is basically sound — or that you can fix any problems without undue cost. Remember, rotting wood will not be made stronger with a lovely stenciled pattern.

Next, prepare your surface well. If it is already painted, you will need to remove the old paint layers with a good paint stripper. Fill any holes and sand the entire piece until it is quite smooth. If it is not painted, you should still make sure the surface is clean and free of wax or polish and that there are no holes or cracks.

Which style of painting you choose is up to you. Stenciling lends itself very well to furniture and it is remarkably simple to achieve a very good result. Freehand painting requires a little more effort but the results are very rewarding.

The charming wicker chair opposite was quite solid but very drab until its facelift. First it was sprayed with two cans of white aerosol paint, using three light coats to give a good covering. The roses were first drawn on with a soft pencil and then painted with acrylic paints. You will need to mix colors to get this range of shades, using the darker ones to give depth to the design and the lighter ones for highlights.

TOY CHEST

A battered pine chest receives a new lease on life with this wonderful painted design of friendly animals. As a special touch, personalize your painted chest with the name of the owner. If you want to hand it down from generation to generation, paint in the family name and you have the makings of a family heirloom which will be loved by generations of children.

MATERIALS

pine chest
steel wool
paint thinner
sandpaper
soapy water
rag
tracing paper
pencil
transfer paper
stylus
black fine felt-tip permanent marker
masking tape
acrylic paints in suitable colors,
*   including black and white*
old dish or plate for a palette
suitable paintbrushes
clear gloss varnish

Below: Transferring the design to the toy chest
Below right: Painting in the design
Right: The completed toy chest

INSTRUCTIONS

See the design on the Pull Out Pattern Sheet.

1 The surface of the chest should be absolutely clean if the paint is to adhere properly. If there is any wax on the wood, remove it by rubbing with the steel wool dipped in paint thinner. Wipe off all the grime and rubbings with the rag dipped in soapy water.

2 When the wood is quite dry, sand the chest all over, inside and out.

3 Trace the design from the Pattern Sheet on tracing paper. You will need to adjust the size of the design to suit the size of your own toy chest. The simplest way to do this is on a photocopying machine. Using two elements of the design, say the smallest and the biggest, work out an appropriate enlargement to suit you. If you do not have access to a photocopier, use the grid method described on page 7 to enlarge the design.

4 When you have a drawing of the right size, tape it in position on the toy chest, using masking tape. Slip a sheet of transfer paper between the drawing and the wood surface and go over all the outlines with the stylus, transferring them to the chest. On a wood surface these markings may be quite faint. If so, you can go over them with the pencil or the fine felt-tip marker.

5 Draw the name in the space provided.

6 Using the old dish or plate for your palette, mix up some paints with a little black or white to add tonal variation to the flat colors. Paint the designs.

7 When the paint is completely dry, strengthen the outlines, whiskers and facial features by drawing over them with the felt-tip marker.

8 Paint one or two coats of clear gloss varnish over the whole chest to protect the painted design. You will see how the colors come to life with a coat or two of varnish.

SPONGED CABINET

Transform an old cabinet, long past its prime, with a wonderful painted effect and new china handles painted to match. Before you begin working on your transformation, make sure that the cabinet is solid – don't waste your efforts on furniture that is about to fall apart.

MATERIALS
an old cabinet
newspaper
paint stripper
scraping tool
detergent
wood filler
sandpaper
wood primer
undercoat
2" paintbrush
water-base paints:
   base color (light)
   second color (medium)
   third color (darkest)
ceramic paint for the handles
natural sponge
plain white china handles
fine paintbrush

INSTRUCTIONS

1 You will first need to remove the old finish and for this step it is important to work in a well-ventilated room. Remove the old handles and spread plenty of newspaper on the floor. Use the paint stripper following the manufacturer's instructions.

2 Wash down the cabinet with a mild detergent-and-water solution. Fill any holes with wood filler.

3 When the cabinet is dry, sand it all over until it is quite smooth.

4 Apply a wood primer and then an undercoat, following the manufacturer's instructions. Allow the surface to dry between coats.

5 Apply the base coat (light color) with the 2" paintbrush and allow it to dry.

6 Wet the sponge and squeeze out any excess water, leaving it just damp. Dip the sponge into the second paint color, dabbing any excess paint off on some scrap paper. Dab the paint on. Do not cover the surface with this color but leave plenty of gaps for the third color.

7 After cleaning the sponge, apply the third color in the same way, filling in the gaps and overlapping the sponging already in place.

8 While the cabinet is drying, you can decorate the new china handles with the ceramic paint and the fine paintbrush. Choose any design, such as flowers, leaves or ribbon garlands. If you need inspiration, china patterns on plates and cups are a good source of designs.

Right: Removing the old finish

*Top: Sponging on the
third color
Above: Painting the
new china handles
Right: The completed
cabinet*

MARBLEIZED PLANT STAND

A good marbling effect can be quite difficult to achieve so it is a good idea to practice on a spare piece of wood until you are happy with the result.

MATERIALS
plain wood pedestal
wood for practicing on
primer and/or undercoat
black matt or low-sheen premium
  paint
white matt or low-sheen premium
  paint
glaze
paint thinner
paintbrushes, one small round, one
  2½"-3" and one fine artist's brush
soft cloth
stipple brush
clear varnish
brush for applying varnish

INSTRUCTIONS

1 Apply primer and/or undercoat following the manufacturer's instructions.

2 Paint the pedestal with the black matt or low-sheen premium paint. Allow to dry.

3 Mix a white glaze consisting of 20% white matt or low-sheen premium paint, 20% paint thinner and 60% glaze. Dab on this white glaze, using the 2½"-3" brush. Don't completely white out the black background, but allow some of it to show through.

4 While the white glaze is still wet, dab over it with the soft cloth, crumpled. This should soften any hard edges and spread the white glaze.

5 Continue to soften the glaze by working over it with a stipple brush and the soft cloth dipped in paint thinner.

6 Mix a little black glaze using the same proportions of paint, glaze and paint thinner as for the white glaze. Using this and the fine paintbrush, draw in some veins. Make them quite irregular and broken, and soften any hard edges with the stipple brush.

7 Using the white glaze and the fine paintbrush, draw in some white veins and stipple as before.

8 When the paint is dry, apply a coat or two of clear varnish to give the glossy appearance of marble.

Above right: Painting the pedestal
Right: Applying the white glaze

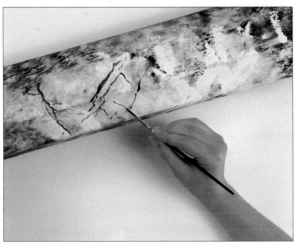

Top: Dabbing off some of the white glaze
Above: Painting in the veins
Right: The marbleized plant stand

Special Effects

Special paint effects were once the province of skilled professional decorators – but not anymore! You can texture and color your walls, woodwork and furniture yourself in ways that will make them unique.

The rough, cold cement floor of the living room, pictured opposite, now looks and feels like expensive inlaid stone blocks, costing nothing but your physical labor and a few cans of paint. A room, apparently paneled in silk, is, in fact, painted to appear that way. Pale, subtle color glows in soft dragged lines on surfaces which previously were flat and dead and of no interest. With your labor, some paint and a lot of enthusiasm, you can turn your home into a treasure house of color, texture and warmth.

The color and pattern you choose can add that magical and often missing element of style to a room's color scheme.

These finishes are suited to articles made from just about anything – wood, glass, ceramics, highly glazed pottery, leather and plastic. Plastic items bought straight off the shelf from a supermarket or department store can be very successfully transformed and made stylish with a painted finish.

So many of the everyday objects that surround us can be completely re-created using painted finishes – old placemats, vases and tin canisters to name just a few.

They create wonderful illusions and the overall effect can look luxurious and very expensive, yet the process can be as cheap as the cost of the paint!

DRAGGING

You can achieve broken color finishes by using two very basic methods: a paint glaze is either added over a background color with a sponge or by spattering; or the paint glaze is rolled or painted on to the background color and then partially removed using rags, combs, stippling brushes and so on. Different tools produce quite different effects with the paint – and the way you manipulate each tool is all-important.

The technique of dragging is perfect for doors, baseboards and moldings. If working on such architectural wood, use a 2" slanted brush (house-painter's brush). A plain door can be transformed into a paneled piece, simply by masking out each panel, dragging and then moving on to the next section.

MATERIALS

*oil-based glaze: one part matt/flat
    enamel to one part glaze
    to one or two parts
    paint thinner
water-based glaze: two parts acrylic
    paint to one part water-based
    glaze (don't use water unless
    the glaze is very thick)
roller to apply glaze
wall-dragging brush with strong bristles*

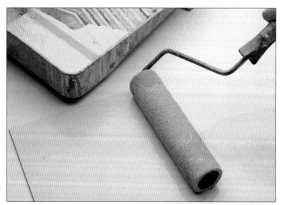

INSTRUCTIONS

1 Dragging requires two people to be working together; one to apply the glaze with the roller and the other to work with the brush. Roll the glaze evenly on to the wall in strips about 1 yd wide. Roll the outside edge constantly so that the glaze doesn't get a dry edge – this will show up as a darker stripe when the wall is complete.

2 Jam the dragging brush into the glaze between the cornice or ceiling and wall and then evenly drag down the wall. If you are on a ladder, just walk down the ladder without hesitating – hesitations will cause irregular stop-marks in the finish.

3 As you work down towards the baseboard, feather the brush out, away from the wall. Wipe the brush, turn it over to the other side, jam it into the glaze at the baseboard and pull it up the wall over the same area you have just dragged down.

4 Feather away from the wall as you approach the cornice. This should be enough for good, strong drag marks. Continue around the room until each wall has been dragged.

*Top: Use a paint roller to apply the paint evenly before dragging
Left: Join the dragging brush into the glaze, feathering the brush out away from the surface you are working on*

RAGGING

MATERIALS

base coat
oil-based top coat
paint thinner
brush or roller
lint-free cotton rags

METHOD

This is a very quick and effective way to achieve an interesting effect on a plain wall, using a scrunched up, lint-free rag or even a plastic bag.

1 You may find some team effort worthwhile here, as the effect depends on the top coat of paint being "lifted off" just after it is applied. While one person is painting the top coat, the other member of the team can follow behind doing the ragging. If the top coat is allowed to dry too much, the effect will be spoiled as not enough of the base coat will show through after ragging.

2 Just after the top coat is applied, it is "lifted off" by dabbing with a rag or something similar, exposing the base color and creating an interesting crushed effect. The base coat can be of emulsion or acrylic paint, thinned with water. You can contrast colors or tones of the same color, by applying a top coat that is darker than the base.

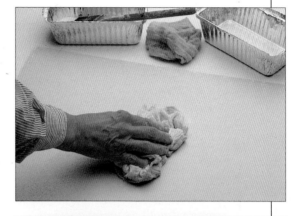

Left: Apply the darker color to the surface to be painted

Left: Before the paint dries, break up and lift off the color using a scrunched-up rag
Below: The rough concrete floor and plain walls of this room have been transformed with special painted effects, including ragging and dragging

CHEST OF DRAWERS

This simple pine chest of drawers was sealed with shellac, painted cream and then a crackle finish applied. The top has a faux marble finish, adding the perfect finishing touch.

MATERIALS
*eggshell finish enamel
masking tape
matt/flat acrylic paint
crackle medium
brush and/or roller
plant sprayer and water
oil-based or water-based varnish*

INSTRUCTIONS

1 The chest of drawers must be prepared with as many coats of background color in eggshell finish enamel (or eggshell acrylic) as are needed to make the surface quite opaque. It is essential that the background not be porous and that the background paint be absolutely dry before the crackle medium is applied.

2 If you intend to use the crackle medium as an inset, such as on

*Right: You can apply this same decorative finish to any unpainted and unvarnished furniture
Far right: The chest of drawers with its lovely crackle finish drawers*

these drawers, first mask out the area with masking tape.

3 Once the tape is down (always run your thumbnail along the edge to ensure good bonding), apply the crackle medium. The crackle medium is viscous and should be allowed to flow onto the surface rather than be painted on in the normal manner. Make sure that the piece is horizontal, as the medium runs if it is on an angle and can make a mess. Allow the medium to dry. This can take from one to two hours to overnight, depending on the weather. Don't proceed to the next step until you are sure the medium is absolutely dry (it dries very flat and is often hard to see).

4 The paint used over the crackle medium must be matt/flat acrylic. You can use acrylic paint, but sometimes good quality artists' acrylic colors are even better. Often a deep-tint base paint will not crack so well because it is too heavily pigmented. You need to try your paint and medium on a sample scrap of wood first. If you want coarse graphic crackling, use the paint straight out of the can, with random

brushstrokes. There must be no pressure on the brush. Let the loaded brush glide over the crackle medium. Keep reloading the brush. Crackling occurs in the direction of the brushstokes.

5 If you want the fine, cobwebby crackling to show, thin the paint: approximately two parts paint to one part water. Once you place the loaded brush, or roller (for ease of application in this instance), on the dried crackle medium surface, it must merely glide over the surface and be reloaded constantly. Speed is of the essence. So, very quickly apply the loaded brush to the surface, keep reloading and reapplying, using absolutely no pressure. Having applied the paint all over, lightly spray three to four times with a fine mist of water from a plant sprayer.

6 The crackling occurs as the paint dries, which is almost immediately. If you wish to protect this finish, use oil-based or water-based varnish. Water-based varnish can reactivate the crackle medium, so be careful not to overwork it. However, once dry and matured for a few days, water-based paint is very strong and, unless the piece of furniture receives a lot of wear, it is not necessary to varnish it.

CRACKLE FINISH WALLS
A fabulous crackled, aged surface can be obtained on walls by using this medium. To be held satisfactorily on a vertical surface, the medium must be thinned: one part crackle medium to one part water. It can then be painted onto a nonporous wall and will dry without running.

The big trick with this wall finish is that the acrylic paint which is used

over the top of the medium must be thick, otherwise crackling will not be effective over the thinned crackle medium.

Once the medium is absolutely dry, the acrylic paint may be applied. It looks best if random brushstrokes are used and, again, the brush must glide over the surface so that the crackle medium beneath is not disturbed. In this case, the paint should be applied with a brush, not a roller. Crackling usually occurs in the direction of the brushstrokes, so bear this in mind as you work. Don't forget to remove the masking tape with a blade, or you will peel the finish off the wall.

Far left: First mark out the area for crackling with masking tape
Above right: Apply crackle medium, followed by a mist of water
Right: Remove the masking tape with a razor blade

EGGSHELL FINISH

Once the surface has been properly prepared, you can begin to apply the painted finish. The first step is to apply as many coats of eggshell finish as are required to produce a totally opaque foundation for the next step. Eggshell finish enamel can be either oil-based or water-based and is quite easy to mix yourself, using the formula given on page 10.

Stenciled Rooms

Stenciling is one of the oldest decorative effects and can be as simple or as ornate as you wish. One of the most effective ways to use stenciling is as a wall decoration and it is so easy to do.

Traditionally, stencils were cut from oiled cardboard or even brass sheets, and were regarded as a craftsman's tools. Today, you can still use brass and cardboard stencils, but inexpensive plastic stencils are now readily available in an enormous variety of contemporary and traditional designs. You can also design and cut your own stencil using a plastic sheet and tracing your chosen design with a china marker or a fine, indelible, felt-tipped pen. (See page 7 for information on how to make your own stencils.)

It is important to use the correct brush for stenciling – an ordinary paintbrush will not do. Stencil brushes are flat topped and are used by dabbing or pouncing the brush down onto the area to be colored, rather than stroking. This prevents paint being pushed under the stencil edges and smearing the design.

It is best to use acrylic or special fast-drying stencil paint. If you are mixing colors to achieve a desired tint, mix enough for the entire room, as it is difficult to duplicate a particular color mix. Take care too that your paints are very creamy in consistency, so they will not clog the brush or sponge, but not so thin that they will run under the stencil edges.

If you are stenciling with more than one color, it is a good idea to cover with masking tape those parts of the stencil design to be painted in the second color. Wait for the first color to dry before stenciling with the second one and so on.

STENCILED BEDROOM

Transform a dull room into a little girl's delight with some very inexpensive touches. The stenciled bluebirds and trailing bows are repeated on the walls, bed, chest of drawers and even give new life to an old wicker chair.

If you are really enthusiastic, you can stencil some bed linen and even floorboards in the same bluebird theme.

The same design has been used for all the stenciling, with adaptations to the basic design to suit the particular angle or surface where it is to be used. For example, the stenciled border that travels up the chimney wall uses only the right-hand bird from the original design, with the upper wing omitted.

BED SWAG

Add a touch
of romance
with this simple
bed swag,
highlighted with
bows and
stenciling.

MATERIALS

water-based paint in white and sky
    blue
large brush
damp cotton cloth
electric drill
3 brass screw hooks
approximately 18 yds white sheer
    fabric
5$\frac{1}{2}$ yds of $\frac{3}{4}$" wide peach satin ribbon
masking tape
white sewing thread
tracing paper
pencil
sheets of clear acetate for the stencil
fine felt-tip permanent marker

sharp craft knife
old dish or plate for a palette
quick-drying stencil paints or acrylic
    paint in blue and peach
stencil brush

INSTRUCTIONS

See the design on the Pull Out
Pattern Sheet.

1   Paint the wall with the white
water-based paint. Allow to dry.
Mix up a pale blue wash by diluting
the sky blue water-based paint. Using
the large brush, swish on the pale blue
to give a soft streaky effect. If some
parts are too strong, lighten them by
lifting a little of the color with the damp
cloth while the paint is still wet. Allow
the paint to dry thoroughly.

2   Find the center point on the wall
approximately 5 ft above the bed.
Drill a pilot hole at this point, then
screw in a small brass hook.

3   Find the center of the 18-yard
length of fabric. Gather the fabric
gently at the center and tie a bow of
satin ribbon to hold the gathering in
place. Let the ends of the ribbon trail.
Tie a second bow to the hook and then
around the fabric to create a double
bow with four trailing ends. Trim the
ends at various lengths, cutting them at
an angle.

4   Mark a point on either side of the
bed, approximately 12" below
the center hook. Experiment to find
the right point by gathering and
draping the fabric. Drill a pilot hole at
each of these points and insert the
brass hooks.

*Above right:
Securing the
sheer drape
Right: Stenciling
the bluebird design*

Left: The bed swag

5 On the fabric, mark with tape equal distances on either side of the center where the drape finishes. As before, tie two satin bows at each of these points, attaching the fabric to the hooks. Remove the tape.

6 Hem the muslin at an appropriate point. You can have it ending just above floor level or have it "puddle" up luxuriously on the floor.

7 Trace the individual bluebirds from the Pattern Sheet on a sheet of acetate with the felt-tip marker. Cut out the stencil with the craft knife. Tape each one to the wall above the center hook. Place a little paint on the old dish or plate. Remove the fabric before you begin painting. Paint in the stencil design. Clean the stencils in water several times while you work as they become clogged very easily.

8 Make a separate stencil for the bow in the same way as for the bluebirds. Stencil the three birds with trailing ribbons around each of the side hooks and one more bluebird below each hook as shown. Always make sure the paint is dry when lifting and moving stencils to their next position.

9 When all the paint is dry, replace the fabric swag.

WICKER CHAIR

This lovely old Lloyd Loom chair has been stenciled with bluebirds, but the wall stencil would have been too delicate for the texture of the chair so a stencil with more dramatic effect has been chosen.

Below: The completed wicker chair
Right: Spraying the first stencil
Below right: Adding the second color

MATERIALS
white wicker chair
spray paint in white, blue and peach
tracing paper
pencil
3 sheets of clear acetate for the stencils
fine felt-tip permanent marker
sharp craft knife
paper for masking
masking tape

INSTRUCTIONS
See the design on the Pull Out Pattern Sheet.

1 First spray the chair all over with blue. Allow to dry. Do not attempt to cover the white background completely.

2 Trace the three stencil designs from the Pattern Sheet onto three pieces of acetate with the felt-tip marker. Cut out the stencils.

3 Tape the bow stencil on the center back of the chair. Tape paper around the stencil to mask the rest of the chair. Spray the stencil in a peach color. It is best to spray several light coats from about 12" away until the wicker is well covered but not clogged with paint.

4 Tape one bluebird stencil on the left-hand side of the bow. Mask around it as before. Spray the stencil in white as for the bow. When the paint is dry, carefully remove the stencil. Paint the bluebird on the other side in the same way.

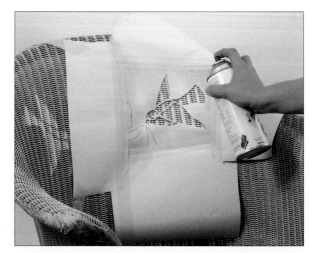

CHEST OF DRAWERS

MATERIALS
chest of drawers
tracing paper
pencil
sheets of clear acetate for the stencils
fine felt-tip permanent marker
sharp craft knife
paper for masking
masking tape
old dish or plate for a palette
fast-drying stencil paints or acrylic
   paints in blue and peach
clear varnish

INSTRUCTIONS
See the designs on the Pull Out Pattern Sheet.

1 If your chest of drawers is looking a little battered, you will need to give it a couple of coats of white, water-based gloss paint before you begin stenciling.

2 Trace the large bow from the Pattern Sheet on a piece of acetate, using the felt-tip marker. For the smaller bow, trace the design from the Pattern Sheet on tracing paper. Sketch in another loop on the left-hand side of the bow. Turn this bow slightly so the ribbon tails hang vertically. Transfer the design to another piece of acetate, using the felt-tip marker. Mark the position of the bluebirds on both sides so you can align them properly when you come to paint them in. Cut out the stencils using the craft knife. Make a bird stencil in the same way. If you have already made a stencil with usable parts, simply mask off any area you do not wish to use.

3 Mark the center of each drawer. Place a little paint in the old dish or plate. Position and paint the stencils as shown in the photograph, cleaning and flipping over the stencils as necessary. Take care not to lift and move the stencils until the paint is completely dry to avoid smudging.

4 When all the stenciling is complete, paint the chest with a coat of clear varnish.

This is another well-used piece of furniture that has been given a new lease on life. You will need to adapt the stencil used for the bed swag for the smaller bow on the second drawer. The larger bow is given on the Pattern Sheet and the bluebird is the one on the right above the bed swag.

Below left: Cutting out the stencils
Below: Painting the stencil on the drawers

WALL BORDER

A dainty border is a pretty feature on most walls and especially those where there are interesting nooks and crannies to be emphasized. Border stencils, such as this one, look most effective along baseboards, chair rails, below window ledges, or along cornices.

MATERIALS
pencil
ruler
sheets of clear acetate for the stencils
fine felt-tip permanent marker
sharp craft knife
masking tape
old dish or plate for a palette
fast-drying stencil paint or acrylic
*   paint in peach, terracotta and blue*
stencil brush

INSTRUCTIONS
See the design on the Pull Out Pattern Sheet.

1 Trace the bluebirds from the Pattern Sheet on the acetate with the felt-tip marker. Trace part of the peach bows, using a dotted line, to help you position the design later on. Mark the top and side lines to use as registration marks for lining up your design accurately. Cut out the bluebird stencil with the sharp knife. Make a separate stencil for the bows in the same way, marking the top and sides as before.

2 Rule a faint horizontal line in pencil on the wall where you wish the top of the stencil to fall. Line up the top mark on the stencil with the pencil line on the wall. Tape the stencil in place. Place a small amount of peach paint in the saucer. Paint in the peach bows with a dabbing motion. Let dry.

3 Lift off the bow stencil and tape it in the next position, using the registration marks you have drawn. Continue until you have finished the entire border of bows. Clean your stencil frequently to prevent it clogging with paint.

4 When the paint is nearly dry, dab on some terracotta color with a clean brush at the points where the ribbons twist and overlap to give a three-dimensional effect.

5 Work along the border with the bluebird stencil and blue paint in the same way as for the bows, matching registration marks and the dotted lines. Clean the stencil frequently as you work.

Left: Use the wall border to accentuate interesting corners

RIBBON BOWS

MATERIALS

sheet of clear acetate for the stencil
fine felt-tip permanent marker
sharp craft knife
pencil
masking tape
old dish or plate for a palette
fast-drying stencil paint or acrylic
   paint in peach and terracotta
stencil brush

INSTRUCTIONS

See the design on the Pull Out
Pattern Sheet.

1 Trace the stencil design from the
   Pattern Sheet on the acetate
with the felt-tip marker. Cut it out.

2 Mark on the wall the position of
   the top of the picture. Remove the
picture. Tape the stencil, centered
above the picture, so that the ends of
the bow trail down behind it.

3 Place a little peach paint on the
   palette. Paint in the design.

4 When the paint is nearly dry, dab
   on some terracotta color with a
clean brush. Do this where the

ribbons twist and overlap to give a
three-dimensional effect. Blend the
terracotta color into the peach so there
are no sudden color changes.

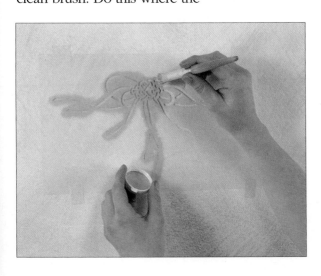

Above: The ribbon bow
Left: Stenciling the peach color

STENCILING A BORDER

MATERIALS
suitable paint
stencil brushes
manila cardboard
linseed oil
paint thinner
sharp craft knife
cutting mat
pencils
plumb line
spirit level
chalk
masking tape
old dish or plate for a palette

METHOD

1 Make the stencil as instructed on page 7.

2 Paint the wall in the normal way. Then, using the plumb line and level, mark the position of your border, marking both the horizontal and vertical base lines.

3 Place the stencil on the wall, aligning its edges with the drawn lines and marking each corner of the

Below: Stenciling in the first color
Far right: The stenciled wall border has been echoed in other parts of the room

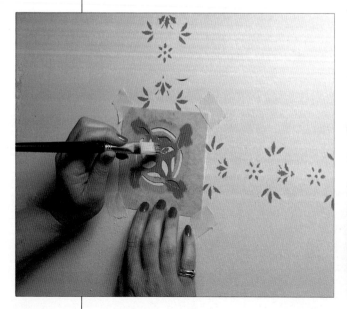

stencil with easily removed blackboard chalk. Continue placing the stencil along the guidelines, marking the corners along the entire length of the border.

4 Attach the stencil to the wall with masking tape. If you are using more than one color, cover any areas to be painted in another color with masking tape to avoid paint bleeding from one area into the next.

5 Be sure to remove any excess paint from your brush or sponge before applying it to the wall. You will find that surprisingly little paint is needed. Work in circular movements from the center of each cut-out area to the edges. Part of the charm of a stenciled decoration is the variations that occur. So don't feel compelled to paint

until a solid block of color appears, or to match one motif exactly to the next.

6 When the paint is dry, unmask the stencil and clean it, if necessary. Then move the stencil to the next set of chalk marks and paint as before. Continue in this way until the border is completed.

Stenciling in the second color

Stencil around a window for added interest

This is an ideal situation for a stenciled "wallpaper" effect. Paint the wall below the chair rail in a color to complement the stenciling.

WALL PATTERN

MATERIALS
long ruler
pencil
sheets of clear acetate for the stencils
fine felt-tip permanent marker
sharp craft knife
string and weight for a plumb line
masking tape
old dish or plate for a palette
fast-drying stencil paint
stencil brush

INSTRUCTIONS

1 Work out how far apart you wish to have the motifs – approximately $3^{1}/_{2}$" apart vertically and 3" apart horizontally looks good. For tight corners, you will need only one or two motifs on the stencil, but it will obviously speed up your work in the larger areas to have six or eight motifs on the stencil. Consider cutting two stencils – a small and a large one.

2 Trace the motif from this page on to the acetate with the felt-tip marker. Draw in horizontal and vertical

registration lines to help you align the stencils. Draw in with dotted lines the other motif outlines. Cut out the stencils with the craft knife.

3 Find the center of the wall and, using the plumb line and a long ruler, lightly mark a vertical pencil line from the ceiling down to the chair rail.

4 Tape the stencil to the wall with masking tape, lining up the first vertical row of motifs with the pencil line on the wall and placing the first motif about 2" from the ceiling. Check that this gives you sufficient room (approximately 5") above the chair rail for the border. You may need to adjust the spacing slightly.

5 Place a little paint in the dish or plate and begin painting in the stencil with a dabbing motion to give a soft grainy texture. If you are using a small two-motif stencil, overlap the lower one you have just painted with the upper one on the next section to space the rows correctly.

6 When the paint is dry, work the next vertical row of stencils, matching up the dotted lines with the painted motifs. Continue stenciling, adjusting the spacing slightly to allow for awkward corners or uneven rows. Stencil up to 5" of the mirror's edge. If there are any large gaps near the curved surface, it is best to leave these until you have painted the border and then add in another motif where necessary.

Right: Cutting out the stencil
Far right: The stenciled hallway and table

Follow these steps to ensure that the border follows exactly the curve of the mirror or table.

HALL TABLE

MATERIALS
tracing paper
large sheet of white paper
pencil
sheets of clear acetate for the stencils
fine felt-tip permanent marker
scissors
sharp craft knife
masking tape
old dish or plate for a palette
fast-drying stencil paints or acrylic
    paints in white and blue
stencil brush
paper towels
clear varnish

INSTRUCTIONS
See the design on the Pull Out Pattern Sheet.

1 Trace the exact curve of the table onto the large sheet of white paper.

2 Trace the design from the Pattern Sheet on sheets of tracing paper. Cut slits alternately in the top and bottom of these tracings so that they can bend. Tape the border design over the curved traced line on the white paper, bending it to fit.

3 Lay the acetate over the top of the design on the curved line and trace in the adapted design with the felt-tip marker, extending and shortening lines as necessary. Cut one stencil for each color to be used, based on this adapted design. Mark dotted registration lines and the curved line of the table's edge on both stencils.

4 Tape the "white" stencil in place and dab in the white paint to make a soft grainy effect. Leave to dry before removing the stencil.

5 Tape the "blue" stencil in place, matching dotted lines and registration marks. Dab in the blue color, using very little paint on an almost dry brush (remove excess paint with the paper towels) to give the subtle mottled finish. Leave to dry before removing the stencil.

6 Paint the table top with a coat of clear varnish.

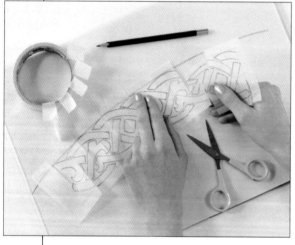

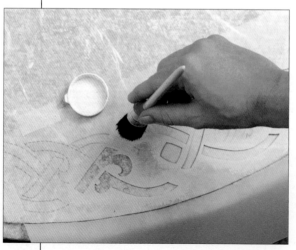

Above right: Cutting the curved tracings
Right: Stenciling in the first color on the table

MIRROR BORDER

1 Trace the design from the Pattern Sheet on the acetate with the felt-tip marker. Cut the bottom edge of the stencil so it will run along the chair rail and make the stenciling job much easier. Tape the stencil in place and paint as for the table border.

2 When you reach a corner, lay a piece of masking tape across the corner at 45° to miter the corner. Paint up to the tape on both stencils.

3 Make a curved stencil in the same way as for the table top. Paint the curved mirror frame in the same way and then paint the straight sides, mitering the corners at the bottom to match up with the rest of the border.

Top: The mirror border
Above: Stenciling in the second color on the table

STENCILED BATHROOM

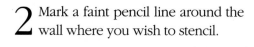

Is your bathroom quite functional but a bit drab? This wall stencil can be reduced to one-fifth of its size to decorate a pile of fluffy towels or a pretty flounce around the sink.

WALL BORDER

MATERIALS
water-based interior house paints in
    white and yellow
brush or roller
damp natural sponge
pencil
ruler
old plates or dishes for palettes
sheets of clear acetate for the stencils
fine felt-tip permanent marker
sharp craft knife
cutting mat (optional)
masking tape
fast-drying stencil paints or acrylic
    paints in yellow, dark pink and
    green
small sponges

INSTRUCTIONS
See the stencil design on the Pull Out Pattern Sheet.

1 Paint the walls white and then, using the large damp sponge dipped in the yellow interior paint, dab paint onto the wall in an even manner. Take care not to have too much paint on the sponge.

2 Mark a faint pencil line around the wall where you wish to stencil.

3 Make two stencils – one for the flowers and one for the leaves. Trace the flowers from the Pattern Sheet on one sheet of acetate with the felt-tip marker, drawing in the leaves with dotted lines. Cut out the flowers. Make a second stencil for the leaves, marking in the flowers with dotted lines. Cut out the leaves.

4 Tape the flower stencil in position on the pencil line. Using a small sponge and the yellow stencil paint, dab in the color around the outside of the flowers. Dab in the pink color at the flower centers, blending the pink with the yellow. Stencil the flowers all around the wall in this way, linking the stencils by matching up the dotted lines.

5 In the dishes or plates, mix up several shades of green, from lime to emerald, by combining the yellow and green acrylic paints in different proportions. Tape the leaf stencil in place at the first position, matching the dotted lines to the flower outlines. Dab in the green, varying the shades of green over the design to add interest. Apply the color lightly to blend in with the sponged effect on the wall.

Left: Sponging the walls with yellow
Above right: The stenciled bathroom
Right: Stenciling in the first color
Far right: Stenciling in the second color

To set off your stylish new bathroom, trim a set of towels with a stenciled fabric strip to match the walls. Highlight the colors of the stenciling with bands of satin ribbon.

TOWEL

MATERIALS

towel
strip of smooth white cotton fabric, approximately 8" wide x width of the towel
pencil
ruler
sheets of clear acetate for the stencils
fine felt-tip permanent marker
sharp craft knife
cutting mat (optional)
masking tape
paper or fabric for masking
fabric paints in yellow, dark pink and green
old plate or dish for a palette
stencil brush
satin ribbon in two colors, twice as long as the towel is wide plus 1½"
matching sewing thread

INSTRUCTIONS

See the designs on the Pull Out Pattern Sheet. Reduce to fit.

Right: The stenciled towels and bathmat, made in the same way as the towels, using the larger stencil

1 Make two stencils – one for the flowers and one for the leaves. Trace the flowers from the Pattern Sheet, drawing in the leaves with dotted lines. Draw in a horizontal line at the top and bottom for registration lines. Cut out the flowers. Make a stencil in the same way for the leaves, drawing in the flowers with dotted lines.

2 Mask your work area with paper or fabric. Tape the cotton fabric strip to the masking.

3 With the ruler and pencil, draw in a faint horizontal line 2" from the top edge to match up with the line on the stencil.

4 Tape the leaves stencil on top of the fabric strip, matching lines. Paint the leaves in a mixture of yellow and green. Allow the paint to dry before lifting the stencil and taping it in its new position, matching dotted lines and registration marks. Complete the border of leaves in this way.

5 Using the flower stencil and working in the same way as for the leaves, paint the outside of the flowers in yellow. For the flower centers, blend in dark pink paint. Allow to dry. Set the paints following the manufacturer's instructions.

6 Trim the stenciled strip along the pencil lines. Stitch the stenciled strip along the width of the towel, turning under the raw edges at both ends and stitching them down.

7 Pin a length of satin ribbon over the raw edges of the fabric strip and stitch it in place. Stitch another length of ribbon parallel to the first.